Disclaimer

Although the author and publisher have made every effort to ensure that the information in this book was correct at publication, the author and/or publisher do not assume and hereby disclaim any liability to any party for any loss, damage, or disruption caused by errors or omissions, whether such errors or omissions result from negligence, accident, or any other cause.

Introduction

It is a fact that we are living in a modern world and we get a lot of advantages and disadvantages for it. One advantage that we shouldn't take for granted at all is the use of social media. It allows us to reach people from all places. It is very important that you have to know the facts about certain social media because there are things that might get you in trouble in the long run, especially if you don't know the things about it.

With all the social media applications that are coming out for our betterment, we actually find it hard to distinguish which is better. The thing is, it will be all up to us to choose on which application we are most comfortable with. In this book entitled "Pinterest for Beginners: A Quick Guide to the Basics", we will learn more about Pinterest. It will teach us what social media is all about. It will guide us on how we should start using the application and we will get the most benefit out of it.

Now, just sit back and relax as you read each chapter of the book. May you find all the learning that will be most beneficial for you.

Chapter 1
What Is Pinterest?

We are now living in a modern world and we are now making use of computers, internet and social media for our own advantage. Before anything else, it would be better if we get to know one social media application at the base level. It will provide us with all the necessary background that will help us as we go further. Pinterest is actually one social media that allows you to express your thoughts and desires through pictures and images. It's essentially an image sharing platform where members 'pin' images to their own 'pin board'. This can be anything you want - it can be random things that you just have an interest in and want to share or it can be multiple images relating to a passion you have. For example you could have a passion for 1960s British roadsters, old company logos, classic men's watches or even a holiday home you really need to hire out. As a member you are able to browse subjects and if you discover a board that you're interested in you then 'follow' it in the same way you do on Twitter and you will be notified whenever any new photos are uploaded to the board. You can also leave comments and join in discussions on each of the images that appear on the site.

Well if you run a business which is selling or producing items which will benefit from good images such as clothes, photography, accommodation, artwork, this looks like it's a terrific opportunity to create some boards to advertise your services because your photos are able to have links back to your own websites product pages. The most beneficial long-term approach from a sales perspective would be to be a part of the community spirit for a little while prior to 'hard-selling' your products, for example 'pin' some non-business pictures and then over time add your items.

If we take the holiday cottage letting example I mentioned earlier, it might be somebody owns a cottage they want to let in Wales for the eight or nine months of the year it's not being used by them. They have a problem on Google because the first 4 or 5 pages of results are dominated by the large letting agents & so they get a board on Pinterest and fill it with pictures of the cottage itself. They also upload images of the surrounding countryside; local places of interest and then wait for other Pinterest subscribers to come across the board, follow them and, ultimately, rent the cottage.

Much like Facebook & Twitter before them though if they keep going at this pace of growth it's only a matter time before everyone's talking about Pinterest. You would probably ask yourself whether we have time to log onto another social media site but this one's definitely different & it's very simple to use so it may possibly fill a gap we weren't aware we had. From a business perspective it's another no-brainer - if you have a service which will potentially benefit from a lot of visitors seeing images of what you are selling you need to be on Pinterest.

Chapter 2
How To Use Pinterest

Pinterest is a social media site that's growing in leaps and bounds. It's been called the 'visual Twitter' because it's all about images. You create boards and share your images with other users. While it may be good for traffic, its real power is how you can use it for branding. For us it's all about using all the marketing avenues available to us to promote our online activities and naturally social media plays a part in that and will grow substantially over the coming years. However, a word of caution here: don't let the other more traditional methods slip, article marketing, blog and forum commenting are still vital - it's all about doing little and often across as many promotional platforms as possible.

First of all, it's important to understand Pinterest's users. When the site started out, it was overwhelmingly young and female. Businesses that catered to that demographic posted pictures of their clothes, fashions, hairstyles, cute pets, food, travel destinations and more. But now it's much more than just young ladies who are using it. So, why do people use Pinterest? They're not there to hang out like Facebook or to network like LinkedIn, and they're not looking for written content. What people mostly do is use Pinterest to relax, take a break and look at some cool images. For marketers, this means we need to avoid hard sell tactics at all costs and content needs to be visually appealing.

On Pinterest, you create 'pin boards' where you put your pictures. Each of your pin boards is based around a common theme. One simple thing you can do with your boards is use them to show off your products. You can create one for each product line. Another way to use them is to find images that your fans would enjoy and post them, kind of like sharing images you've found. This is good for business niches because you can show info graphics. For the self-help niche, you can pin images with inspirational quotes. Like all social media sites, Pinterest is all about engaging your audience. You've got to do that as much as possible.

You can ask for opinions, get comments going, and conduct surveys with a free giveaway. There's a cool feature offered by Pinterest that can really get your fans involved.

Another engagement idea is to get your fans to take a picture and post it on your board. It could be a picture of them with your product or those doing something related to your brand. When Pinterest started out, like all social media sites, nobody knew if it was going to go anywhere. Now it looks like it's here to stay and if you don't get on board, you'll miss the train.

Chapter 3
How To Upload Videos And Images To Pinterest

While other social platforms also allow posting of images, with Pinterest you have the added advantage of categorizing your images into various "boards." This gives followers the opportunity to hone in more narrowly on their specific interest. If you're an organization with many products and styles, the platform gives you a way to narrow things down for your potential customers. The instant gratification of the right image lends itself beautifully to the online contest. By creating a site that asks people to share images of a selected topic, and to offer an incentive for posting, such as a prize or coupon, you have the ability to draw interest for your brand or organization. You can encourage people to create a board based on their favorite images from your site, and then broadcast that whoever gets the most pins and repins, wins.

Once you've held your contest and drawn in some new followers, you're now beset with another monumental task -- but one that can yield monumental rewards. Its research and this is something that every social media manager should take seriously. By monitoring the things being repinned from your boards, you have the ability to conduct research into the habits, interests and behaviors of your audience, and to tailor your future efforts toward what's been popular in the past. Pinterest has another purpose for those who spend a lot of time online and need some place to file away all their great ideas for later use. Whether you're an educator, marketing expert or photographer, the ability to add items you love to your boards allows you organization ideas on-the-fly, with little fuss. They'll be readily accessible when you need to retrieve them. On top of that, you have social features working in the background; posting ideas on your board means that even while you've left your boards idle, you may have others repost those images, or share even more images with you that pertain to that topic.

Pinterest also has potential for educators. Think about the traditional yearbook that students spend the whole year agonizing over -- which is really a collection of memorable photos with some captions included. If you're a journalism teacher, yearbook adviser or other type of educator, you could use Pinterest as a forum for student collaboration. If you're creating a yearbook, a group Pinterest board could be a place to throw out ideas or consider certain photos. If you're in charge of a student newspaper, Pinterest could be an online extension of the newspaper's brand. For photography students, you could create a board for students to share photos or images that pertain to a certain theme. As a general rule, ensure that your pins give credit where credit is due by "pinning" from the original site, as opposed to Google Images or another aggregation service.

Chapter 4
How To Get Pinterest Followers

One of the new social media craze is the pinterest and it will be best that before you start using this, you will be aware of how to get pinterest followers. With all the social media applications we have, it is hard to get hold of all of them. It is then important that you get techniques so that it will be easier to handle your followers from one social media to another. The first thing you can do is to tie up your existing social network with your Pinterest account. One of the fastest and easiest ways to get more Pinterest followers is by tying your account to your existing Facebook and Twitter profiles. Doing so means that every new item you pin will be displayed to your followers on these networks. Since you already have established connections with subscribers on these sites, you'll find that many of them elect to follow your Pinterest profile naturally.

Another you can do is to make your account easy to pin. Integrating Pinterest buttons into your blog posts, product pages and other areas of your site can help boost the number of times your content is pinned and lead to new followers for your profile. Because Pinterest is still relatively new, simply having these buttons in place provides a visual reminder for people to subscribe to your profile and engage with your content on this new site. You can also create boards to supplement your post; doing so makes your content more engaging and gives readers a reason to follow your profile.

It is important that you should pin regularly because this will help you find the ideal balance between posting titles that have no value. For best results, aim to pin between 5-30 new items a day, depending on the number of active Pinterest boards you maintain. Then you can try to improve your board naming structure, this will help you follow the boards that are most relevant to them, it's important that your board names make it immediately apparent what each of your boards are about.

People love tutorials, and the unique visual display of Pinterest makes it ideally suited to create tutorials that other users can follow. As an example, say you run a site that teaches affiliate marketing to website owners. Using Pinterest, you could create a "step-by-step" tutorial board, in which you feature links to different articles from around the web on topics like choosing affiliate products to promote, building traffic to your site and improving conversions. Create tutorials on topics that you know will interest a number of people and you're sure to pick up more followers for your account. One of the ways that people find new Pinterest users to follow is by searching the site for interesting key phrases in order to uncover new pinned content.

Chapter 5
How To Follow Others On Pinterest

Pinterest is the latest social networking site to be created. Here, users can upload photos and create collages based on their interests. Business owners may also use the site to post items and follow other users. A Pinterest mass follower utility can help increase traffic to the business's website. This works in a very similar manner to Facebook and Twitter. Individuals and business entities create their accounts and begin posting to their boards. Other users can access these boards and view the posts made. This is made easier by following those users whose posts match one's interest.

Through the use of a mass follower utility, business owners are able to enter a keyword or keywords and have the bot search through all the different entries on Pinterest and automatically follow those accounts. This occurs much faster than a human could sort through the posts and follow them. This bot should also enable the user to collect interesting posts from other users based on the keywords entered and mass repost them. This will make all these posts accessible to those users following the business's posts. This will keep the content on the business pin board new and interesting.

In addition to mass following users whose posts contain certain keywords, this bot is also capable of collecting public information about these users. This includes user IDs collected from user pin boards and comment threads. One interesting phenomenon seen on Pinterest and other social networking sites is the fact that most users will follow those users who follow them. Users believe that their shared interest will be better served if information flows both ways. This is generally proven to be true.

What this means to users of a follower utility is that they will grow a large network of followers in practically no time at all. A large number of those whose accounts the bot chooses to follow will automatically follow them back. This opens them up to receiving your marketing message. This is good for a business because there is no doubt that these followers are interested in the particular product or service being marketed. That makes them almost twice as likely to click through to the website being promoted and see what is being offered.

The simple truth is that finding the best Pinterest mass follower utility will help one reach a far larger audience and generate more traffic on their website in a shorter time than any other form of advertising. Pinterest is free to users, as are other social networking sites. It has a large and growing number of users more than willing to share their experiences with a business, good or bad. Thus, it is easier for you to get followers.

Chapter 6
Pinning Videos On Pinterest

To pin your videos, you'll first need the short link that leads directly to your video on YouTube.com. It's easy to get that, the first thing you should do is to find your video in YouTube.com and simply click the share button. Click on the small Options drop-down menu near the bottom-right of the shortened embed code. Check the box marked "HD Link." Copy the short "youtu.be" code in the slim box. Don't use the embed code. The next you should do is to head on over to Pinterest.com. Then you have to click the Add + link in Pinterest. Paste your shortened link and click "Find Images." You should also try selecting your video board. Be sure to write a description in the text box. You can copy and paste your YouTube video description to this text field. Lastly you should start clicking "pin it".

Pinterest is a great way to share expertise, especially in the DIY, crafts and cooking categories. A contractor could create a huge following with a video series of simple household repair tips. If you're a realtor or an interior designer, Pinterest is a great place to show off a beautiful home. Landscapers can also show off their work. A great way to take advantage of the social aspects of Pinterest is to create a collaborative board. If you're connected with your friends, customers or stakeholders, add them to a collaborative board and invite them to post their videos.

If you have a brick and mortar store, encourage customers to shoot a quick video of the product they've just bought. Reward those who share their videos on Pinterest or who add content to your collaborative board. If you embed a lot of videos on your website or blog, ask visitors to pin your video. Many Pinterest users have browser plugins that allow them to easily pin website content. As you produce your videos, keep Pinterest in mind. You may find yourself making videos exclusively for Pinterest. Don't be afraid to ask people within your video to re-pin it after they've watched.

As Pinterest continues to grow and evolve, video content will become more common-place. Now is the time to get in on the ground floor. Learning the things about Pinterest is actually fun yet challenging. You will definitely enjoy this one kind of social media which provides you with very many good things as a user. It is true that many people have taken advantage of such social media. It will be a wise decision on your end as an entrepreneur if you will utilize every social media available. This will definitely lead you to acquiring as many viewers as you want to help your business grow.

Chapter 7
How Fast Is Pinterest Growing?

Pinterest is regarded as an extensive simulated pin board. The creators' goal is to be able to let people worldwide connect with each other through all the things that may interest them together. This is a great way for people to bond with one another via shared pursuits and preferences. Through Pinterest, you can manage and share everything that you find good, fascinating, and beautiful on the internet. Users utilize the pin boards to organize their current projects, concerns, and ideas such as home decorating ideas, wedding plans and designs, personal fashion preferences, work-related inspirations, free recipe collections, and others. There are about 32 various topics that Pinners can check out and make use of. The best thing about Pinterest is that, since it's a social site, Pinners can also look into the pin board that was created by others. Surfing other people's pin boards is a fun and interesting way to learn about new ideas and things about anything and everything that you have any interest in.

For instance, if you are interested in art, you can check out the said category and look for pin boards that other people pinned so that you can acquire the latest art-related news and ideas, and so on. The most important words or phrases to learn if you want to enter the world of Pinterest are 'pin' and 'board'. Pin is the term used for every image that is put into Pinterest while board is a collection of such pins. Pinterest allows all users to add countless pins as many as they want. You can also follow all the boards of a particular Pinner or just follow a certain board that you are interested in.

Furthermore, you will realize that like any other social media account it has grown in numbers swiftly. Its users vary from businessman to teenager who loves to try new things. It is important that you'll get a good background of what this is all about so that you will have a good idea of what you should expect. True enough, you will get a lot of benefit as you use Pinterest for your own interest. You can get a lot of followers that will lead you to your success.

It will also allow you to post a lot of good things that you would like others to see. It is true that this type of social media gives a lot of impact to society. Thus, it creates a lot of good impressions. In the end, you will realize that there are a lot of good things coming for us with our technology. It is true that Pinterest has grown a lot when it comes in numbers and users.

Chapter 8
Creating Your Boards On Pinterest

The World Wide Web is flooded with social blogs and social sharing websites. Thus, building a social blogging platform and capturing the attention of the web users and becoming popular is not a cake-walk. Innovation and intuitiveness only can help you stand out of the crowd. Pinterest is such an innovation. It has fascinated the social bloggers and network geeks, which eventually increased its user base world-wide. The highlighted feature of this visual online pin board is its invitation-only hordes. With many trying to replicate the idea, a ready-to-execute solution to start running the social network websites helps to stay ahead of the curve.

Pinterest clone scripts have started popping up all over the web and hence choosing a good script in the big sea is a crucial task. Look for the rich and the best script that renders all inevitable and essential features and incomparable user-interface. Below are the necessity criteria to check while finalizing on a Pinterest clone script.

A Pinterest clone script developed in an open source framework. You should be able to create a social pinboard that allows users to upload images, videos and URL. Allow users to enroll only upon invitation. Show Pin-It button to create boards, Follow button to follow users. Easy to use interface, allowing users to create any number of boards, upload any number of pins. Social sharing features like Email and Tweet to pin favorite pins, login using Facebook account and Twitter account, Invite friends of Facebook network and Twitter network. Account management facility- Allow users to manage their own account like edit profile settings, manage boards and pins, find friends, invite friends and view self-activities done recently. The Joomla Pinterest clone website should deliver a common page displaying all popular pins on the page. Quick menu options will help you to browse through various categories of the social pin board.

Show the most liked pins / most repinned pins in the popular column. Comfortable and easy search options to find pins, boards and people are available. Admin management facility - Complete control over the entire pin board, add new members upon accepting the invitation, manage each pin that is uploaded by the users, manage categories, site settings as well as user account. The Pinterest clone script for Joomla should come as 100% unencrypted source code with completely customizable interface, ensuring a capability to enhance the social sharing website in future as per user needs. A Pinterest clone script that just mimics the present layout does not feed the needs. Choose a Pinterest clone that has an eye-pleasing unique design and innovative features that is capable of attracting a large user base and giving you wild success. In the end, you will realize that there are a lot of things that you have to learn so that you will enjoy Pinterest.

Chapter 9
Reasons For Downloading Pinterest Adder

One of the new sites that has gotten a lot of attention and is showing rapid growth and popularity is Pinterest. This web site lets users add videos and images with an easy to use interface. The content is then displayed in a fashion that is similar to the way people pin things onto a bulletin board. You can quickly add some relevant pins, like pins automatically and follow others with a Pinterest adder, or as it is sometimes known, a Pinterest robot. The idea of using social media sites as a business marketing tool to promote businesses, services or even a personality is now commonplace for large and smaller companies. Social media itself is constantly evolving as new web sites come onto the scene, and people who want to remain current will have to keep up with the times.

Each person can put their pins in various categories, or boards as they are called on the site. Each one of these boards have a theme and contain pictures from that category which can be used to organize images and ideas and can also make it easy to navigate for others who might want to follow the board. Each one of the categories can represent something related to the user's interests or business. Adding content is necessary for business users as it keeps their page fresh, informative and relevant. Though it is easy to add content, it can be somewhat time consuming as well. To help solve this problem, users can use a marketing robot to help them add content; generate traffic to their site and to gain leverage in the social media market.

These robots are available through many different Internet companies and at a wide array of prices and features. Some of the businesses give customers the option of downloading a free trial so they can get an idea of how it works before buying it, but most of those people who try them out end-up buying it as they feel it is worth the price. As soon as the Pinterest robot has been downloaded, it can begin work immediately. It can get busy gathering other people's user information, can follow users and like their pins and can also add new pins to boards. Some of them have a feature that allows users to schedule activity which can be a convenient feature for people who want to have new content added consistently. These bots might also have a feature that comments on pins and has the ability to customize various operations.

The robots will help to save the user quite a lot of time, as it can do the work while the user sleeps working or networking. And by having a page that is constantly receiving new material, the user will eventually gain more followers. The more people who follow someone can mean more potential customers who are seeing their products and their info. Social media members should think about buying a Pinterest robot or Pinterest adder. These useful bots are of great help when a user wants to add fresh, relevant content to an account without having to invest the time that it would take to do it manually. It is also very helpful for users who want to attract more followers, likes and potential clients.

Chapter 10
Using Pinterest Robots To Generate Mass Follower

Pinterest is the latest social networking site to be created. Here, users can upload photos and create collages based on their interests. Business owners may also use the site to post items and follow other users. A Pinterest mass follower utility can help increase traffic to the business's website. This works in a very similar manner to Facebook and Twitter. Individuals and business entities create their accounts and begin posting to their boards. Other users can access these boards and view the posts made. This is made easier by following those users whose posts match one's interest.

Through the use of a mass follower utility, business owners are able to enter a keyword or keywords and have the bot search through all the different entries on Pinterest and automatically follow those accounts. This occurs much faster than a human could sort through the posts and follow them. This bot should also enable the user to collect interesting posts from other users based on the keywords entered and mass repost them. This will make all these posts accessible to those users following the business's posts. This will keep the content on the business pin board new and interesting.

In addition to mass following users whose posts contain certain keywords, this bot is also capable of collecting public information about these users. This includes user IDs collected from user pin boards and comment threads. One interesting phenomenon seen on Pinterest and other social networking sites is the fact that most users will follow those users who follow them. Users believe that their shared interest will be better served if information flows both ways. This is generally proven to be true.

What this means to users of a follower utility is that they will grow a large network of followers in practically no time at all. A large number of those whose accounts the bot chooses to follow will automatically follow them back. This opens them up to receiving your marketing message. This is good for a business because there is no doubt that these followers are interested in the particular product or service being marketed. That makes them almost twice as likely to click through to the website being promoted and see what is being offered.

Of those who click through, a very large percentage will go ahead and make a purchase, becoming active customers. If they are completely satisfied with their experience of the website, they will become the best advertisement money cannot buy. They will share their experience with other members of their network and spread your marketing message far and wide. The simple truth is that finding the best Pinterest mass follower utility will help one reach a far larger audience and generate more traffic on their website in a shorter time than any other form of advertising. Pinterest is free to users, as are other social networking sites. It has a large and growing number of users more than willing to share their experiences with a business, good or bad.

Chapter 11
Increase Traffic Generation Through Pinterest

Pinterest is one of the hottest and fastest growing social networking sites on the Web. As such, it is one of the most useful tools available for finding and targeting prospects to view one's marketing message. This site drives more traffic than YouTube, Reddit, Google, and LinkedIn combined. That is the reason a Pinterest bot is an essential tool for increasing website traffic. This program will help you find targeted leads based on the specific keywords you name. It will gather user IDs from public areas of Pinterest such as comment threads, pin boards, and more. It can be set to auto follow other users who show an interest that matches the product or service being marketed.

By mass following others, the bot gains you followers who follow you back. Many of these will then click on through to your website. You can also take a pin from one of your followers and "re-pin" it or share it with the rest of your network. This helps to keep you fresh and in sight of your audience. There is also an auto-like function that searches out pins, boards, and more that match the keywords given. Whenever one is found, the like link is activated, which can tie your network into Facebook and vice versa.

Of course everyone hates spammers. For this reason, one special feature is necessary to have the best bot. That is the ability to move certain IDs to a "black list" and avoid sending them messages if they express a desire to stop receiving them. This feature can also be used to fine tune a marketing message and send it out to only a portion of one's network that has shown greater interest in a particular item while avoiding those who seem disinterested. If one uses a Pinterest bot with all of these features, the odds are that he/she will see a massive influx of traffic to his/her website. Of course, it is then up to him/her to ensure that the site is interesting enough that those who visit will want to come back as repeat customers.

With many followers, you can surely create the traffic you've always wanted. There are actually a variety of reasons why people want to generate as many followers as they can. For the entrepreneurs, they want followers so that many get to follow their posts which will help them promote their business. It is true that a lot of users use social media such as Pinterest so that they can promote their business in the most convenient way. After all, promoting your business online is the easiest way yet very profitable because you'll get to spread your advertisement in a span of time.

<u>Chapter 12</u>
Tips On Building Your Business With Pinterest

Although, Facebook, and Twitter are still the topmost social networking sites in the world as first and second, respectively, there is a new and fast-rising social site that's been making its name these past few months. It's called Pinterest. If truth be told, Pinterest's popularity is so high lately that many online sites are trying to copy their concept and simply put a little twist on it to make it their own. Many people and businesses hadn't caught up with this latest trend in the market so this article should help you get some ideas on what Pinterest is and how you can personally use it or how it can be of use to your business and website.

Through Pinterest, you can manage and share everything that you find good, fascinating, and beautiful on the internet. Users utilize the pin boards to organize their current projects, concerns, and ideas such as home decorating ideas, wedding plans and designs, personal fashion preferences, work-related inspirations, free recipe collections, and others. There are about 32 various topics that you can check out and make use of. The best thing about Pinterest is that, since it's a social site, Pinners can also look into the pin boards that were created by others. Surfing other people's pin boards is a fun and interesting way to learn about new ideas and things about anything and everything that you have any interest in.

For instance, if you are interested in art, you can check out the said category and look for pin boards that other people pinned so that you can acquire the latest art-related news and ideas, and so on. The most important words or phrases to learn if you want to enter the world of Pinterest are 'pin' and 'board'. Pin is the term used for every image that is put into Pinterest while board is a collection of such pins. Pinterest allows all users to add countless pins as many as they want. You can also follow all the boards of a particular Pinner or just follow a certain board that you are interested in.

As you can ascertain from the know-how of Pinterest above, you can add images or pins in your Pinterest account that will feature your services and/or products. Then, you can also include a follow button from Pinterest to your own website. Make sure that your images are interesting and fun to catch the attention of all Pinners because if they are attracted, they can re-pin your images to their own pin boards but you, as the original source, will get some credit for it. And, you should know that re-pins retain the original source-link even if it's repined for numerous times so your website will certainly get attention.

Chapter 13
Promotion Techniques For Pinterest

Pinterest is a visually based social media site that focuses on users interacting based on common interests and visual appeal, rather than social circles. This is where your social media methods must change from your techniques used on Facebook and Twitter. Leave the networking for those sites. Here, you must appeal to what people want- and ideally- what those outside of your social circles want to see.

#1 Showing off your business the Pinteresting way

Pinterest isn't just about working off of a single pin board. There are various topics for you to cover, so make sure that you spread your business across every topic you can. You can even use Pinterest to tell stories of your business, such as the history influences that brought about its present structure. Don't just post items for sale, or pictures of your products and services, because you won't appeal to the "browsing" nature that is present on this media. It's all about the looks here. If you're a local business, create boards with pictures of your city, surrounding areas, and even photography that is unique to your area. Be sure to set the localization of your business to improve local SEO rankings and coverage for your account.

#2 Linking to your sites

Pinterest focuses primarily on pictures and videos, your links must be relayed through images. You can utilize this primarily through your blogs and website, further improving the value that images and videos have on a site's effectiveness. Because of the connective abilities that Pinterest offers, you can link to various sites throughout your network. But remember that your links will draw traffic to a certain site, and this is where you'll have to do your best to impress them. Don't guide traffic to vacant parking lots; draw them to areas where others have already gathered. Pinterest definitely gives you an edge when it comes to directing site traffic, if you do it the right way.

#3 A few things to beware of

No privacy settings. This means that anyone can look at your information and pins. Of course, this is somewhat of a double edged sword, allowing anyone on the internet to find you, but that also leaves you open to spam. While this doesn't seem to be a problem right now, it is something to look out for, primarily comments with irrelevant links posted to your pins. Overall, Pinterest is an excellent business tool in the making. There may still be a few adjustments to be made, perhaps some new interest board topics and other quirks, but for the most part, Pinterest is a social media tool that can definitely boost your businesses online presence that customers will be interested in.

Chapter 14
Using Pinterest To Organize Events

It is easy to keep your ideas in an organized board as you begin planning your event. You can create individual boards with dedicated topics using identifying images. Each aspect of your event can have its own place. When you add the pin it button plug-in to your browser it is quick and easy to post the images your research uncovers. The images you select can be instantly added to your Pinterest pin boards as you navigate to relevant websites. You simply select the appropriate image, choose which board to add it to, provide a simple description and "Pin it."

Visual references in the form of the pins you collect enable you to instantly arrive at the information you have collected. You can reference any topic related to organizing your event, compile a list of vendors to supply your event and mold your events look and feel. Your pins are not restricted to only your Pinterest profile. You can link your profile to Twitter and Facebook making it extremely easy to share your ideas with anyone associated with your project. You can also scroll through the boards other collaborators have placed on their Pinterest profiles and gain more insight to direct your efforts.

As you begin pinning and repinning various items others can follow you. If they become instrumental to your campaign it is a simple prospect to add them to your boards. The inspiration is not limited to only those you are already aware of however. You can follow and be followed by anyone in the world who has a profile on Pinterest. Becoming inspired by other people's pin boards is what Pinterest is all about. There are many themes involved in planning any event. Regardless of how many efforts you must put together, Pinterest has made it a highly efficient process to add and delete any number of subjects to your profile. All of the boards you create will be permanently placed on Pinterest until the time you decide they are no longer needed.

This is especially useful when being involved with organizing recurring events like company picnics or Christmas parties. Editing and sharing your pins with friends is made especially easy with Pinterest. Anyone associated with your project can "like" your pins thus casting their vote on the content you post. Friends and followers become collaborators to your efforts while you- the creator of your boards- maintain control of the content.

When you locate expert information to aid you in organizing your event it is very simple to "follow" them when they are pinned. Find out who the "go-to" authority for your event is and create a board for them exclusively. A wealth of great ideas will be sure to result. You can follow magazines, blogs and professional websites. If your event is public and you need to create interest or generate participation, use descriptive images with popular tags to attract a target audience. Simply select those titles that are associated with the interested parties and their attention will be yours. Compile a variety of subjects or themes in the beginning of your project and allow interested parties to respond. Your audience will define their interest for you and your pre-selected topics will guide your theme. Events are rarely planned by a single individual. Brainstorming is a very effective approach to developing your ideas. Adding images to boards and developing ideas is the favorite activity of Pinterest subscribers.

When you allow your friends or co-workers to pin and repin their ideas, the ideas you've supplied will evolve on their own. If you are working with collaborators it becomes easy to compile a list of pros and cons for any idea suggested. Crowdsourcing is an excellent way to gather inspiration. When you post ideas for the public to respond to, your pinboards will completely fill out. Pin pictures of those who are scheduled and pictures of those you wish to invite and watch your guest list take on a life of its own. It would virtually be impossible to overlook an item of planning when you have highly visible imaged based reminders at your disposal. With those who "follow" and "like" your photos, no idea will be left unexplored. Use the Pinterest board to show people what kind of activities they might expect to see at your event. Making separate boards for each activity will allow for a more comprehensive coverage of your topic.

When your event is over and the participants want to gather photos of the event for their own use there is no other place better suited to share them with those who attended. You will not have to wait for everyone to finally get around to "tagging" their photo to their Facebook uploads.

Chapter 15
Reasons On Using Pinterest For An Event

Making your pins visually compelling is a must if your pins are to be popular. Some of the most followed pinners come from a digital design background. Their pins are bright and colorful. Select your pins to be as visually compelling as possible by carefully selecting those photos, videos and Infographics that are the most gripping. If you create your boards to appeal to a variety of interests among your targeted audience your boards will become a special place to your visitors. They have the option to follow your entire profile or to select specific boards of yours to follow. Pin your images with this in mind to get the results you hope for. You can create special boards to target specific niches.

Pinterest visitors often want to view new pins from people they are not already following. Browsing with a definite category to find the things that interest them is what they do when searching for their interests. Appropriately categorizing your boards will ensure that the right folks find the things you pin. Base your board's category on the affiliated content that accurately represents what your event offers. Use Keywords in Your Descriptions Appropriate keywords allow proper context to lead to desired exposure. Your keywords should embrace the information found in your pin as well as why you pinned it. That will help your pins to be found. That way when someone uses your keyword in the search box your pins will be listed in the results.

Create a Speaker's Board In keeping with conventional social media rules you want to temper the information you pin with relevant content from additional sources beyond your own. By including relevant information that others are pinning relating to your event topic you are sure to not exclude those you wish to attract to the event you are organizing.

In the end, you will realize that using Pinterest will provide you with all your business needs. It will be a lot easier if you use any social media to promote an event you are organizing. Through this, you'll get to reach as many people as you can. You should know that to get people interested in your event, you have to make a lot of promotional campaigns. You just can't consume your time promoting alone. You have to consider preparing for the main event. That is why it will help you a lot if you would promote online because you will not be stuck to promoting it only. You can let the magic of social media work. It will be spread from one account to another. You will just be amazed with the fact that even those you don't know will know your cause.

Chapter 16
Tips On Succeeding In Your Events Through Pinterest

There are actually a lot of ways that you could succeed in organizing your event through Pinterest. Despite that there are ways that you should consider so that you can be assured of all the things that would come your way. Below are the following tips that you should bear in mind to avoid the hustle and bustle of event organizing.

1. VENUES:

Many event organizers work in a variety of locations that include many different settings. Keeping each of these venues on dedicated boards is an excellent way to keep clients apprised of your efforts. Using photos of the places you've been allows them to sort through their options quickly. It is also a good idea to include the capacities of the facility listed so prospective clients can appropriately include or exclude them from their options according to their needs.

2. ATTENDANCE GIFTING:

Attendee gifts can often present a challenge when looking for that unique idea that best represents the theme or purpose of the event being planned. Creating a designated board for this purpose and allowing others to pin their ideas can greatly enhance your selection of the perfect gift to offer. Additional ideas collected on boards can serve for future events to be planned.

3. FURNITURE:

Most companies offering rental furniture have many items to select from. You can create separate boards for tables, chairs, sofas and any other items that may be needed. You can categorize these options to dedicated themes and create a database for future event planning. By saving your favorite choices to their own boards you can avoid having to sift through long lists of items which were previously decided against.

4. <u>INVITATIONS:</u>

Innovative invitations are always among the most challenging tasks for event planners. The beauty in using Pinterest boards to compile your invitation data again lies in the ability of others to contribute their ideas. Pin boards are ideally suited to store the items you absolutely love making them and their providers easy to access for any event. Publicly displaying your invitations when it is appropriate to do so is easily accomplished at Pinterest.

5. <u>FOLLOW UP:</u>

Collecting photos from the attendees after the event is an excellent way to promote your company and your clients as well. There is no better vehicle to use to accomplish this as Pinterest. Use the power of social media to celebrate your event and promote future opportunities.

6. <u>NEWS:</u>

Showcasing your event on blogs and in news articles is an excellent way to promote your efforts within the event planning industry. Pin boards are ideally suited to doing this. You can link your pins back to the landing pages previously created to support your efforts.

7. <u>PORTFOLIOS:</u>

There is no better way to showcase the history, mission statement and vision of your company than using pins of past, present and future events as they are being planned. In keeping with the appropriate SEO techniques you can be sure to promote your brand and attract a loyal following through Pinterest.

8. <u>CREDIT YOUR SOURCES:</u>

It is always important to remember to credit your sources when pinning to the public. Copyright laws are often infringed upon even by those with the best intentions. The surest way to avoid this is to be certain to properly credit your sources whenever using information provided by others.

Chapter 17
Pinterest On Successful Events

Creating a board on the Pinterest homepage is begun by clicking "Add" on the upper-right-hand portion of the page. From there choose the "Create a Board" option. If you are planning an event choose a name that best describes it. Some ideas could include the name of the event and the date it occurs. If you are planning a wedding your choice could include the name of the bride and groom. Be sure to include the specific keywords needed to guide your targeted audience to your boards. Installing many pins to your board will be a regular part of the organizing an event process. Selecting the appropriate images is very important here. Instead of uploading each item from the Pinterest homepage you will want to install the "Pin It" button to your web browser.

This will enable you to pin directly from the site you are visiting without leaving the page you are on. Installing the button involves clicking on the "About" from the Pinterest home page and selecting the Pin It Button option. Display your Bookmarks Bar by clicking View_Toolbars_Bookmarks Toolbar. Now just drag the Pin It Button to your Bookmarks Toolbar. From now on whenever you are browsing on the web simply push the Pin It button to automatically pin the image of you choosing to the board of your choice. Decide on the most important aspects of the event you are planning and dedicate an individual board to each idea. Ask yourself what are the "most important" ideas you wish to include and share with those involved? For example if you are organizing a party some of your categories could include: Entertainment; Food; Music and a Guest List. If your event is a seminar your board titles could include: Speakers; Topics Discussed; Location; Food and Equipment Needed. You could begin by devising a list of categories that you want to develop and create a board for each one. As you begin to pin your ideas you will see the category evolve and develop into a well-organized option to your event.

This is the most fun part of organizing your event. Navigate to relevant web pages that contain the information you wish to include and put your Pin It Button to work. Choose the item you want to include, name it and select the board you want to pin it to. It will instantly be placed on the board. Pinterest offers you the opportunity to view your pin right away or you can see it afterward by visiting your profile page. Continue until your boards are full of the ideas you collect. Inviting collaborators is the final step to setting your event planning in motion. It is rare to organize an event all by yourself and you probably will benefit from the ideas of others. Inviting other pinners to list their ideas to your board will give you additional inspiration and a whole bevy of ideas. Inviting collaborators is easy and fun to do at Pinterest. Choose the board you wish to invite people to and select the "Edit" button at the base of the board. Pushing the "Me and Contributors" option allows anyone you list under "Who Can Pin" to participate in your event planning by pinning images of their own to the board you've selected.

Chapter 18
Pinterest As A Successful Model

Pinterest, the hottest buzz in the tech world at the moment is considered as the new social hit. It has reached the 10 million mark already and Tech savants evaluate it as the most successful innovation after Facebook in recent times. What makes it so captivating? Let us have a deep look on this latest fad. Pinterest is all about social sharing. The website allows its users to create a self-board and pin images, videos or URLs of any interesting things they stumble upon in the web world. It opens up a global platform for its users, letting users to share the things they love/attract, with people of similar interest worldwide. Pinterest works on 'invitation-only' and so one can become a pinner only after sending an email request which upon acceptance will send the activation link, allowing the user to login via their Facebook/Twitter account. Also, the Facebook/Twitter friends can send invites for their network friends to join them in pinning things of similar tastes.

Pinterest has a beguiling interface that gains traction. A user can create unlimited boards in his account, pin any number of images and videos, and re-pin any user's pins that has attracted them. Pinterest is also tapped as a marketing tool for business as one can easily promote their business, connect with their customers, stay active in the Pinterest community by pining, re-pinning, following other boards etc. and thus create a loyal fan base for their brand. Does the phenomenal growth of Pinterest and its obsession among the web users dumbstruck you? So if you want to develop your own Pinterest website and create a unique web presence, there are numerous Pinterest clone scripts popping up over the internet due to the rising demand from new takers. If you have understood well about the Pinterest trends, its strategies and working, a good Pinterest script that bestows a similar interface and features will help you start a Pinterest like website without any hardship.

Currently Pinterest is available by only invitation. It helps the user to share his interesting stuff as visual images. It is a social site which binds users via photos. After the user has created an account and logged in, they will be asked if they need a board in which one can post relevant photos. While surfing the internet if anyone needs to have the photograph from a website means just pin the image by clicking the button pin it. If another user of the site likes your image then they may follow your future pins.

Pinterest has limited application in business because it won't offer any direct advertisement services. Pinterest in future has business models and will be coming out with paid service in a solid user base establishment. Using the multi-channel marketing mix retailers can benefit with highly visual product lines. Pinterest user's image based lifestyle followers so sharing the content with illustration and visual image may reinforce a brand. Pinterest main focus with demographic is to reach with visual nature which fits for retailers. It is incorporated with the brand's larger social marketing strategy. Pinterest offers the customers of the retailers to share the brand content with other online social networks. And the retailer should facilitate their websites with the "Pin It" option. In addition to site optimization the retailers should highlight the offer and discounts to Pinterest referrals.

Chapter 19
Pinterest Frequently Asked Question

There are a lot of applications coming out these days especially when it comes to social media. One of the many things that you can enjoy is Pinterest. It is one social media that you can enjoy just like Facebook and Twitter but like any other application it has certain things that needs to be tackled. With the coming of Pinterest, there are also questions that would come along. It would be best then that you take a look at those frequently asked questions before you start using Pinterest. Through this you will be able to avoid hassles and things will be a lot easier for you. You can visit their website for your own review but before anything else; try looking at these frequently asked questions:

1. <u>How do I create a new board?</u>

You have the option to choose who can pin to your board. You can choose 'just me' or if you'd like multiple contributors, you can choose 'multiple people'. Choosing 'multiple people' will require that you add the other person's username or email address.

2. <u>How do I 'pin' an image from the web onto a board?</u>

There are a couple ways to do this. You can go to the menu bar at the top right of the Pinterest page and click [Add -> Add Pin]. From here, you can enter the URL of the website image and click 'Pin it".

3. <u>How do I search for specific types of images?</u>

You can look for certain types of images by clicking on the 'Everything' link and selecting one of the 18 categories provided such as gifts, food + drink, travel, DIY, kids, etc. Another option is to type in the search field specifically what you are interested in such as 'flower arrangements' or 'Audrey Hepburn'. This should return images where those words were used in the description of the image.

4. <u>How do I rearrange my boards so that my most frequently viewed are at the top (or any other arrangement)?</u>

The pinterest staff has recently added this feature. Go to [Your user name -> Your Boards]. This should produce all of your boards. There is a 'Rearrange' button in the top right corner. Click that button, move your boards in the order you want, and then click save. It's as easy as that.

5. <u>How do I delete a pin or a board?</u>

For either a board or a pin, you should see an 'edit' button when you hover over the image. Click 'edit' and then 'delete (pin or board)' in the new window that appears.

The above questions are just a few of the many things that could come your way. However, you shouldn't be discouraged of the things you will be seeing because this is part of the technicalities of the said application.

Closing

Now that you have learned more about Pinterest, you may have realized that great things come in small packages. Just like this social media application, you can surely have the easiest way to promote your business and flaunt your expertise. You can take the book as your guide so that you will know how things are to be taken.

In the end, you will realize that this book will help you understand the basics of Pinterest and moreover that you will gain the knowledge in how to take advantage of it. You can definitely read on this over and over again so that you will have a deeper realization of what Pinterest is.